So Easy Publishing
Banbury, Oxfordshire, UK

So Easy Publishing is a trading name of ICT So Easy Ltd.
© So Easy Publishing and ICT So Easy Ltd, 2020
The moral rights of all author(s) have been asserted.
First published in 2020.

Acknowl
The autho
their supp ......opment or this
book and throughout his educational career.

Cover image from Shutterstock. Other images are produced by the author.

External links and references:
Wikipedia is free to access at point of publishing. The author and/or ICT So Easy Ltd take no responsibility for the contents therewithin.

This book relies on the use of the paid for service at db.ictsoeasy.co.uk; however the data can be accessed for free from GoodReads and replicated into a free MySQL or MariaDB server installed locally or remotely.

Links to third party websites are provided in good faith and for information only. So Easy Publishing disclaims any responsibility for the materials contained in any third-party website reference in this work.

MySQL – The Basics

Learning Computing One Bit at a Time
Book Six

Contents

All code is tested at db.ictsoeasy.co.uk

Introduction

In the dark annals of time information was stored in filing cabinets, drawers, on desks and occasionally inside the family dog. With the advent of the computer, data was stored in digital files, and eventually the RDBMS or Relational Database Management System was born.

Along with databases, some clever chaps at IBM developed a special language for interacting with databases, a Structured Query Language or SQL (pronounced SEQUEL).

Developers unhappy with a number of things in commercially available systems, the system MySQL was developed and has proven to be one of the most popular RDBMS's.

This book will teach you the very basics of using MySQL. You can install MySQL for free on your own computer, although it is quite large and cumbersome, or you can access **db.ictsoeasy.co.uk** to explore using a real MySQL installation. This is the method that will be used in this book

Exploring a Database

Databases store their data in tables (sometimes called relations). But how do we know what tables we have available? We can enter a command to show all tables that are in the current database. Log on to db.ictsoeasy.co.uk and type in the following command into the SQL code box:

```
SHOW TABLES;
```

Capitalisation is by convention; it will work in lower case but it is good to do things the *right* way. The semi-colon at the end indicates the end of an instruction. If this is the first time you have used the system you will get a single response, something like:

```
Tables_in_db_user_1
```

1 is your user ID; yours will be different. This is a heading in the results, and it is empty for a simple reason: there are no tables in the database at the moment! Let's conduct a bit of a cheat and load a sample dataset. If you choose Datasets and then SimpleBooks, a sample dataset will be loaded into the database for you. This is a sub-set of books from the website GoodReads and will be used throughout this book.

If you run the command again:

```
SHOW TABLES;
```

You will get a different result. This time all of the tables in the database SimpleBooks are listed:

```
Tables_in_db_user_1
```
```
books_simple
```

Now that we know we have a table of data called books_simple, we can explore the table a little bit by describing it. Type the command:

```
DESCRIBE books_simple;
```

And you will be presented with a table of information:

Field	Type	Null	Key	Default	Extra
id	int	NO	PRI		auto_increment
Title	varchar(255)	YES			
Authors	varchar(600)	YES			
Rating	decimal(5,3)	YES			
Language	varchar(40)	YES			
NumPages	int	YES			
PubDate	date	YES			
Publisher	varchar(100)	YES			

Let's understand what the columns mean first:

- **Field** – If you were to organise your data into a table, then each field would be a column. It is a single type of data which each entry into the table has. If it was a table of people, then each person would have a name – 'name' would be a field.
- **Type** – this tells the database how to store the data in it's memory. Different data needs storing in different ways. This will be discussed in more detail later in this book, but here you can see ints (short for integers, or whole numbers), varchars (a mix of letters and numbers), decimals (with a decimal point) and a date).
- **Null** – Null is a special word for nothing. If a field has Null as 'Yes', then that field is allowed to be left blank. If it is 'No' (like the id field) then it *must* have a value or it will give us an error.
- **Pri** – this is short for Primary Key. A primary key is a unique way of identifying a record of data. This will be discussed in more detail later in this book.
- **Default** – this is a value that is set to a field if the field is left blank when it is entered into the database. In this table, we don't want the computer to guess for us so we have no defaults!
- **Extra** – there are a number of other settings that fields can have. In our table, we have set id to *auto_increment*, so whenever we add a new book into the table it will *automatically* be given the next available ID number.

Selecting Data from a Table

The term for looking at data in a database is SELECT, we SELECT data from a table which matches certain criteria. The syntax is SELECT fields FROM tablename; The simplest option for *fields* is to use the wildcard, *, to select everything.

```
SELECT * FROM books_simple;
```

This will select *all* fields from the books_simple table and list them on the screen. The first five rows are shown below.

id	Title	Authors	Rating	Language	NumPages	PubDate
1	Harry Potter and the Half-Blood Prince (Harry Potter #6)	J.K. Rowling/Mary GrandPre	4.570	eng	652	2006-09-16
2	Harry Potter and the Order of the Phoenix (Harry Potter #5)	J.K. Rowling/Mary GrandPre	4.490	eng	870	2004-01-09
4	Harry Potter and the Chamber of Secrets (Harry Potter #2)	J.K. Rowling	4.420	eng	352	2003-01-11
5	Harry Potter and the Prisoner of Azkaban (Harry Potter #3)	J.K. Rowling/Mary GrandPre	4.560	eng	435	2004-01-05

As you will see when you run the code, there are a *lot* of records, and the columns are very long and often unneeded. You can use one of the **Clear Output** buttons to make things more manageable.

We can list just the field names we want to see to remove the columns we don't want. To show just the book title, author and rating we could use the command:

```
SELECT Title, Authors, Rating FROM books_simple;
```

The first five rows are shown below:

Title	Authors	Rating
Harry Potter and the Half-Blood Prince (Harry Potter #6)	J.K. Rowling/Mary GrandPre	4.570
Harry Potter and the Order of the Phoenix (Harry Potter #5)	J.K. Rowling/Mary GrandPre	4.490
Harry Potter and the Chamber of Secrets (Harry Potter #2)	J.K. Rowling	4.420
Harry Potter and the Prisoner of Azkaban (Harry Potter #3)	J.K. Rowling/Mary GrandPre	4.560
Harry Potter Boxed Set Books 1-5 (Harry Potter #1-5)	J.K. Rowling/Mary GrandPre	4.780

Activity 1.1
Try and list the id, title and number of pages for all of the books.

We still have an awful lot of data showing though; it is common to want to see just a sub-set of the data in the table; not just reducing the columns, but also reducing the number of rows returned.

The thing to do is to think 'what question do I want to ask?' and formulate that into the SQL syntax. For example, "What book titles and authors do we have that are published by Random House Audio ?" We could write this as:

```
SELECT  Title, Authors, Publisher
FROM books_simple
WHERE Publisher = "Random House Audio";
```

MySQL doesn't care about us putting parts of the command on different lines, and it makes it much easier to read. In this example we have included "Publisher" in the SELECT clause, but that wasn't part of the question so we can leave that out while including it in the WHERE clause:

```
SELECT  Title, Authors
FROM books_simple
WHERE Publisher = "Random House Audio";
```

We are left with a much-restricted set of results:

Title	Authors
The Hitchhiker's Guide to the Galaxy (Hitchhiker's Guide to the Galaxy #1)	Douglas Adams/Stephen Fry
In Cold Blood	Truman Capote/Scott Brick
The Da Vinci Code (Robert Langdon #2)	Dan Brown/Paul Michael
The Summons / The Brethren	John Grisham/Michael Beck/Frank Muller
Like Water for Chocolate	Laura Esquivel/Yareli Arizmendi
Lolita	Vladimir Nabokov/Jeremy Irons
The Michael Crichton Collection: Airframe / The Lost World / Timeline	Michael Crichton/Stephen Lang/Anthony Heald/Blair Brown
The Stephen King Collection: Stories from Night Shift	Stephen King/John Glover

Activity 1.2
List all of the book titles and their publishers by J.K. Rowling. Be careful about the space after the K.!

You may have noticed that there are fewer books when you completed the activity than you might have been led to expect from the big, long list you first looked at. This is because the = symbol means 'equal to', and it has to be *exactly* the same. If we want to look for *anything* by J.K. Rowling, we can use the LIKE keyword instead.

```
SELECT Title, Authors
FROM books_simple
WHERE Authors LIKE "%Rowling%";
```

This will give you a more complete set of results. Note that as well as replacing the = with LIKE we have included % signs inside the speech marks (we call something inside speech marks a 'string' by the way). The % means 'something or nothing' so %Rowling% means something or nothing followed by Rowling followed by something or nothing, so it would match:

J.K. Rowling   Rowling
Rowling Banks   J.K. Rowling Junior

We can limit our results mathematically against numerical fields as well by using comparison operators. The most common ones are listed below:

Operator	Purpose
=	Is equal to
<	Is less than
>	Is more than
<=	Is less than **or** equal to
>=	Is more than **or** equal to
!=	Is not equal to (sometimes written as <>)
BETWEEN ... AND ...	The data is between two values

For example, the following command:

```
SELECT Title, Authors, Rating
FROM books_simple
WHERE rating > 4.9;
```

Will give you a list of all books rated above 4.9 (there's not that many that awesome!)

Conversely:

```
SELECT Title, Authors, Rating
FROM books_simple
WHERE Rating BETWEEN 3.9 AND 4;
```

Will give you the same list, but only books rated between 3.9 and 4 inclusive. You can also use this format when limiting by date (note: dates are written as YYYY-MM-DD). So:

```
SELECT Title, Authors, PubDate
FROM books_simple
WHERE PubDate > "2010-01-01";
```

Will tell you the Title, Authors and Publication date of all books in the list published since 2010.

Activity 1.4
List the Title, Authors and Publication date of all books that that were published between 2005 and 2006.

Sometimes we need to limit our data by more than one field. We can combine our WHERE clauses using logical operators. These are listed below:

Operator	Purpose
AND	Ensures both sides of the operator are true. Sometimes written as &&.
OR	Ensures one or both sides of the operator are true. Sometimes written as ‖.
NOT	Ensures that the clause is NOT true. Sometimes written a !.
XOR	Ensures either side but *not* both sides of the operator are true.

To list all books written by Terry Pratchett and Neil Gaiman, we would use the code:

```
SELECT Title, Authors
FROM books_simple
WHERE Authors LIKE "%Neil Gaiman%"
  AND Authors LIKE "%Terry Pratchett%";
```

But to find all books either of them have written (regardless of whether they were working together or not) you would change the AND to an OR.

```
SELECT Title, Authors
FROM books_simple
WHERE Authors LIKE "%Neil Gaiman%"
   OR Authors LIKE "%Terry Pratchett%";
```

To Find the books Terry Pratchett worked on *without* Neil Gaiman, we would add a NOT before the first LIKE to negate it (and return to the AND).

```
SELECT Title, Authors
FROM books_simple
WHERE Authors NOT LIKE "%Neil Gaiman%"
  AND Authors LIKE "%Terry Pratchett%";
```

The last thing we need to think about is order. At the moment our results come out in the order they were stored in – not necessarily what we want. We can order by any field we want, in either ascending (increasing) order, or descending (decreasing) order by using the ORDER BY *fieldname* clause followed by ASC or DESC. The following code:

```
SELECT Authors, Title, PubDate
FROM books_simple
WHERE Rating > 4.9
ORDER BY PubDate ASC;
```

Gives you:

Authors	Title	PubDate
Aristophanes/F.W. Hall/W.M. Geldart	Comoediae 1: Acharenses/Equites/Nubes/Vespae/Pax/Aves	1922-02-22
Tara MacCarthy	Literature Circle Guide: Bridge to Terabithia: Everything You Need For Successful Literature Circles That Get Kids Thinking Talking Writing‚Äîand Loving Literature	2002-01-01
Middlesex Borough Heritage Committee	Middlesex Borough (Images of America: New Jersey)	2003-03-17
Julie Sylvester/David Sylvester	Willem de Kooning: Late Paintings	2006-01-09

While changing the ASC to DESC gives you:

Authors	Title	PubDate
Julie Sylvester/David Sylvester	Willem de Kooning: Late Paintings	2006-01-09
Middlesex Borough Heritage Committee	Middlesex Borough (Images of America: New Jersey)	2003-03-17
Tara MacCarthy	Literature Circle Guide: Bridge to Terabithia: Everything You Need For Successful Literature Circles That Get Kids Thinking Talking Writing‚Äîand Loving Literature	2002-01-01
Aristophanes/F.W. Hall/W.M. Geldart	Comoediae 1: Acharenses/Equites/Nubes/Vespae/Pax/Aves	1922-02-22

Inserting Data into a Table

The term for adding new data into a database is `INSERT` and we use the syntax:

```
INSERT INTO tablename (list of fields)
        VALUES (list of values);
```

There are some important rules to remember, however. Strings (text) have to be inside quotes. These can be single quotes or double quotes, but you cannot mix them for a single piece of data: 'this is ok' – "and so is this" – 'but this is all kinds of wrong!"

Most people tend to stick to a preferred choice – in this book we tend to use "double quotes" for readability – but you also need to think of the data itself. 'this "text" works best with single quotes' – whereas "Jo's text works best in double quotes".

You also have to remember to keep dates in the right order – year-month-day. Let's insert a new book. You've probably notice the list is missing a fair bit of Terry Pratchett, which is a crying shame, so let's fix that:

```
INSERT INTO books_simple (Title, Authors, Rating, Language,
                          NumPages, PubDate, Publisher)
VALUES ("The Colour of Magic","Terry Pratchett",3.98,"eng",
        293,"2008-12-26","Transworld Digital");
```

Selecting all of Pratchett's books will now show the book in the results:

```
SELECT Id, Title
FROM books_simple
WHERE Authors LIKE "%Pratchett%";
```

Id	Title
2442	Witches Abroad (Discworld #12; Witches #3)
12070	Good Omens: The Nice and Accurate Prophecies of Agnes Nutter Witch
12071	Buenos Presagios: las buenas y ajustadas profec√≠as de Agnes La Chalada
12221	The Colour of Magic

Note that we ignored the id field in our insert? This is because it was set to auto_increment and you can see it has added in it's own new id number. You *could* leave other fields out as well, if needed, as NULL was set to YES for the other fields. This means if you didn't know the number of pages, for example, you could leave that out by just not listing the field.

Now you could go ahead and enter all of Pratchett's books like that, and we absolutely advise you read them first, but it is quite painful building up the query time after time. Instead, you can insert multiple items at once by separating the values list with commas:

```
INSERT INTO books_simple (Title, Authors, Rating, Language,
                          NumPages, PubDate, Publisher)
VALUES ("The Light Fantastic","Terry Pratchett",3.96,"eng",
        277,"2002-02-02","HarperTorch"),
       ("Equal Rights","Terry Pratchett",4.01,"eng",
        240,"2005-01-15","Harper Perennial"),
       ("Mort","Terry Pratchett",4.21,"eng",
        243,"2001-02-06","HarperTorch");
```

Activity 2.1
Find some of your favourite books on goodreads.com and add them in to the database. Try both the single insert and the multiple insert method.

Changing Data in a Table

Mistakes happen, especially when you're all excited from reading a Terry Pratchett book. You may – if you are a fan – have noticed the misspelling above; Equal Rights should in fact have been Equal Rites – which is a pune or play on words[1].

We need to correct this, but of course databases don't work like a word processor, you can't just click and change, you have to UPDATE the data. The syntax for this is:

```
UPDATE tablename
SET field = newvalue
WHERE somefield = somevalue;
```

Now you might think the easiest way is to use:

```
UPDATE books_simple
SET Title = "Equal Rites"
WHERE Title = "Equal Rights";
```

---

[1] This also is a Pratchett-based pune or play on words – see https://wiki.lspace.org/mediawiki/Pune

This absolutely will work but is a bit of a pain. Particularly the text you're trying to correct is long and convoluted. It could also be, of course, that there is another book by a different author that actually *is* called Equal Rights.

However, if you think back to what we learnt before, we have *id* as a primary key. A primary key is used to uniquely identify a row, or *record,* of data. So we could do a SELECT statement to find the id...

```
SELECT *
FROM books_simple
WHERE Title LIKE '%Rights%';
```

id	Title	Authors	Rating	Language	NumPages	PubDate	Publisher
131	The Power of One: The Solo Play for Playwrights Actors and Directors	Louis E. Catron	3.670	eng	240	2000-07-02	Heinemann Drama
10232	Pathologies of Power: Health Human Rights and the New War on the Poor	Paul Farmer/ Amartya Sen	4.250	eng	438	2004-11-22	University of California Press
12224	Equal Rights	Terry Pratchett	4.010	eng	240	2005-01-15	Harper Perennial

Now we know the correct id, 12224, we can use *that* in our UPDATE statement:

```
UPDATE books_simple
SET Title = "Equal Rites"
WHERE Id = 12224;
```

You can be a bit more creative with your updates to fix problems. For example, if we select a distinct list of languages using the clever DISTINCT keyword, you will see that there are quite a few variations of English listed:

```
SELECT DISTINCT language FROM books_simple;
```

language
eng
en-US
fre
spa
en-GB
mul
grc
enm
en-CA
ger
jpn
ara
nl
lat
por
srp

There is no need for en-US, en-GB etc, English is English, so we can use a LIKE in our WHERE clause to change anything that starts with en- to "eng":

```
UPDATE books_simple
SET language = "eng"
WHERE language LIKE "en-%";

SELECT DISTINCT language FROM books_simple;
```

(Notice how we wrote two commands there? MySQL is fine with this! The line break is just for readability.) Your new list should be much shorter with just 'eng' listed.

You can be even cleverer by writing some mathematical commands inside the update statement. For example, if you run:

```
SELECT Title,Authors,Rating
FROM books_simple
WHERE Authors LIKE "%Pratchett%";
```

You will see some silly people – probably Internet trolls or the like – have somehow rated some of Pratchett's books as less than 4! We can write an UPDATE statement to add 1 to all of the ratings of Pratchett's books. We can also add an extra clause in the WHERE to make sure that we only add it to those *under* 4 (else we will end up going over 5 which is the maximum). These three lines will make the change, but also show you the difference.

SELECT Title,Authors,Rating
FROM books_simple
WHERE Authors LIKE "%Pratchett%";

UPDATE books_simple
SET rating = rating + 1
WHERE Authors LIKE "%Pratchett%" AND Rating < 4;

SELECT Title,Authors,Rating
FROM books_simple
WHERE Authors LIKE "%Pratchett%";

Activity3.2

Shakespeare – while a decent playwright - has somehow been rated higher than Terry Pratchett. Unbelievable! Update the database to set the rating of anything that is by Shakespeare and has a rating of 4 *or higher* to be reduced by 1. Don't forget to list the results before and afterwards to check the changes.

WARNING Databases don't (generally) have an undo button. Always be super careful with any update (or deletc) queries as a mistake can have dire consequences! ICT So Easy won't be liable if you have to go back to the start of the book and begin again!

Deleting Data from a Table

Sometimes there is just data we no longer need. In this case we have to DELETE the data from the table. There's not a lot new to learn here, the syntax is:

```
DELETE FROM tablename
WHERE fieldname = somevalue;
```

The WHERE clause can be built up just the same as in the previous queries. If you were to list all of the book details, you would see there are some books such as id 249 which look a bit odd:

id	Title	Authors	Rating	Language	NumPages	PubDate	Publisher
249	Tropic of Cancer	Henry Miller/Ji≈ô√≠ N√≠1	3.680	eng	318	1994-06-01	Grove Press

These odd characters are because the data is in some format we can't display. We could try to figure out an Anglicised version, but let's just delete it instead shall we?

```
SELECT *
FROM books_simple
WHERE id = 249;

DELETE FROM books_simple
WHERE id = 249;

SELECT *
FROM books_simple
WHERE id = 249;
```

Should result in the book, showing, then the line `Query OK, 1 row affected.` to show the data has been deleted, and then an empty list being shown.

Activity4.1
Records 288 to 291 also have problems. Delete them all!

Of course, as the WHERE clause is just like in the previous queries, we can do some more clever things with it; for example, we could delete anything with a rating less than 1 (because they must be rubbish and not in our database!)

```
SELECT *
FROM books_simple
WHERE Rating < 1;

DELETE FROM books_simple
WHERE Rating < 1;

SELECT *
FROM books_simple
WHERE Rating < 1;
```

Activity4.2
You know what, I'm still a bit upset by Shakespeare trying to take all of the limelight from Pratchett! Delete all of the Shakespeare books!

Creating a Table

We've pretty much come as far as we can with a single table of data – there are other things you can do but we've covered the important bits. Well done! Let's review some of the key terminology:

Data: a single 'thing' we know.

Datatype: an instruction to the database about how to store the data.

Record: a collection of data about a single entity such as a person. This can be thought of as a *row* of data.

Field: a single piece of data (in each record) of a single data type. 'First name' would be a field.

Table: a collection of data about a common topic organised into fields and records.

Primary Key: A field which can be used to *uniquely* identify a record of data.

Query: an instruction, written in SQL, and consisting of clauses to perform an action on a database.

RDBMS: A system which manages related data across tables and manages the SQL queries.

Hang on a second… across tables… what?

We've not dealt with that bit yet have we? Our table is actually a bit rubbish at the moment. Data should be *atomic* – split into the smallest bits possible. This means that if there is a change (such as referring to 'English' rather than 'eng' in the languages column) then only one change needs to happen and therefore there will not be inconsistencies throughout the table.

The biggest problem is the authors, but that's a bit out of the scope of this book as many authors can write many books and many books can have many authors. Another area which has repetition, however, is the language.

What we want to do is split the database into two tables, one for the books and one for the languages. We can then build a relationship between them. As each book can only have one language, but each language can be used in many boos we have what is called a "one to many" relationship, which we can draw like this:

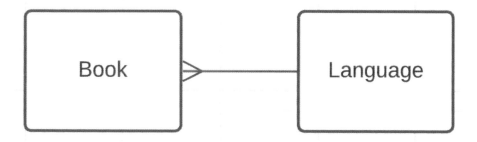

The "crows foot" demonstrates the "many" part of the relationship. There are other notations for the "entity relationship diagrams", though this is possibly the simplest.

Creating a table uses the syntax:

```
CREATE TABLE table_name (
    column_name datatype,
    column_name datatype
    ...
);
```

Remember we discussed data types right at the start of the book? These are simply a description of the data so that MySQL knows how to store it properly. The language is stored in the current table as a VARCHAR(40). VARCHAR (Variable Characters) is just database speak for "text" and the 40 shows the maximum length we will allow. As this is the current format, we may as well keep it the same. We will also give each language an ID number so we can refer to it. As this will be a whole number we will use INT (integer) and we will ask MySQL to AUTO_INCREMENT it – this means it will set the first one to "1", the second to "2" and so on. As the ID number will be our unique way of identifying a language, then we will make that the PRIMARY KEY. We can also include a new column, a description of the language, which we will make text again, but a bit longer, by using VARCHAR(255). The language field should not hold duplicate values, so we can set it to be UNIQUE. So our table creation code will look like:

```
CREATE TABLE languages (
    id int AUTO_INCREMENT PRIMARY KEY UNIQUE,
    language VARCHAR(40) UNIQUE,
    description VARCHAR(255)
);
```

Running SHOW TABLES; will show your new table has been created. Of course, you will need to add the descriptions yourself using UPDATE commands.

Of course, you now need to get all of the languages from the books_simple table into the languages table. Of course you can list them all and use a lot of INSERT commands if you wish, but we can write a clever piece of code to select all of the existing data and insert it automatically:

```
INSERT INTO languages (language)
SELECT DISTINCT language FROM books_simple;
```

If you now do `SELECT * FROM languages` you will see your updated table. Hurrah!

Finally we need to make the link from our books_simple. Really this should be done when we first setup our database, but as we are *editing* our table we'll use a few cheats. We need to:

Add a column in the books_simple table to hold the language id

Find the corresponding key for each language in the books_simple table from the languages table and add it in.

Delete the existing languages column in the books_simple table.

The code to do this is:
```
ALTER TABLE books_simple
```

```
ADD COLUMN language_id int;

UPDATE books_simple
SET language_id = (
     SELECT languages.id
     FROM languages
     WHERE languages.language = books_simple.language);

ALTER TABLE books_simple DROP COLUMN language;
```

Don't worry if you don't fully follow all of this code, it's a means to an end so that you have a working database to play with for the final section!

Activity 5.3
Add a publishers ID to the books_simple table, add in the ID's from the publishers table and then remove the existing publishers field from the books_simple table.

Selecting Data from Multiple Tables

The tasks from the previous sections, splitting our table into multiple tables and making our data more atomic, is known as normalising. Our data isn't fully normalised because of those pesky authors, but it's close enough for this book.

But now we have a problem; if I want to know all the information about book 10 (the Harry Potter Collection), then when I `SELECT * FROM books_simple WHERE id = 10;` I get a most unhelpful series of results:

id	Title	Authors	Rating	NumPages	PubDate	Language_id	Publisher_id
2	Harry Potter Collection (Harry Potter #1-6)	J.K. Rowling	4.730	3342	1994-06-01	1	2

How do I actually find out what the language is? (or the publisher, for that matter?) I have to do a multi-table selection. The first thing I need to do is include both table names in the FROM clause:

`SELECT * FROM books_simple,languages WHERE id = 10;`

Now we know we are selecting everything from every table. But this gives me an error:

Error: (1052) Column 'id' in where clause is ambiguous

Theres is a field called "id" in both tables, so MySQL doesn't know which one has to be equal to 10. We can fix the correct table by using *table_name.field_name* in the WHERE clause. That should do it:

```
SELECT *
FROM books_simple,languages
WHERE books_simple.id = 10;
```

Uh-oh. We won't print that out here because it would take about three pages... What's happened is MySQL has gone through and listed every combination of the results from the SELECTing everything from `books_simple WHERE id = 10` (one line) and SELECTing everything from languages with no WHERE clause (sixteen lines). 1x16 = 16, so we get 16 results.

To fix this we need to add *another* clause in WHERE stating that we *also* want the results to only be shown when the language ID in books_simple is the *same* id used in languages. We do this using an AND.

```
SELECT *
FROM books_simple,languages
WHERE books_simple.id = 10
   AND books_simple.language_id = languages.id;
```

Activity 6.1
SELECT all the information about the book " The War of the Worlds",
including the publisher details.

Activity 6.2
Try and extend Activity 6.1 to include all publisher *and* language information
about War of the Worlds. This is a challenge!

Results can get quite big quite quickly, so it's a good idea to only select the information needed. Although you can get away with skipping table names when there is no duplication, it is a good idea to include them anyway. However, this can lead to *very* long queries so we can use shorter table names (often just the first letter) by using the AS command:

```
SELECT b.title,b.authors,b.numpages,l.language
FROM books_simple AS b,languages AS l
WHERE b.id = 10
   AND b.language_id = l.id;
```

Activity 6.3
Using the AND command, find just the author names, title, language and
publisher of The War of the Worlds.

Solutions to Activities

1.1
```
SELECT Id, Title, NumPages
FROM books_simple;
```

1.2
```
SELECT Title, Authors
FROM books_simple
WHERE Authors LIKE "%Rowling%";
```

1.3
```
SELECT Title, Authors, Publisher
FROM books_simple
WHERE Publisher LIKE "%Audio%";
```

1.4
```
SELECT Title, Authors, PubDate
FROM books_simple
WHERE PubDate BETWEEN "2005-01-01"
                AND "2006-12-31";
```

1.5
```
SELECT Title, Authors, NumPages, Rating
FROM books_simple
WHERE NumPages < 100
  XOR Rating > 4.91;
```

2.1
This will be dependent on the books you choose. However, the INSERT statements should match those shown in the examples.

3.1

```
SELECT DISTINCT Publisher
FROM books_simple;
```

There are a range that could be combined using UPDATE statements, for example the first two are "Scholastic Inc." and "Scholastic". Doing:

```
SELECT DISTINCT Publisher
FROM books_simple
WHERE Publisher LIKE "%Scholastic%";
```

Will show even more, all of which could be combined using:

```
UPDATE books_simple
SET Publisher = "Scholastic"
WHERE Publisher LIKE "%Scholastic%";
```

3.2

```
SELECT *
FROM books_simple
WHERE Authors LIKE "% shakespeare%";
UPDATE books_simple
SET Rating = Rating - 1
WHERE Authors LIKE "%shakespeare%"
  AND rating >= 4;
SELECT *
SELECT *
FROM books_simple
WHERE Authors LIKE "% shakespeare%";
```

4.1

One solution would be:

```
DELETE FROM books_simple
WHERE id = 288;
```

And then changing the 288 to 289, 290, and 291. Alternatively you could combine them into one query:

```
DELETE FROM books_simple
WHERE id = 288
   OR id = 289
   OR id = 290
   OR id = 291;
```

But most effectively would be to use BETWEEN:

```
DELETE FROM books_simple
WHERE id BETWEEN 288 AND 291;
```

4.2

```sql
SELECT *
FROM books_simple
WHERE Authors LIKE "%Shakespeare%";

DELETE FROM books_simple
WHERE Authors LIKE "%Shakespeare%";

SELECT *
FROM books_simple
WHERE Authors LIKE "%Shakespeare%";
```

5.1

```sql
CREATE TABLE publishers (
    id int AUTO_INCREMENT PRIMARY KEY,
    publisher VARCHAR(100) UNIQUE
);
```

5.2

```sql
INSERT INTO publishers (publisher)
SELECT DISTINCT publisher FROM books_simple;
```

5.3

```sql
ALTER TABLE books_simple
ADD COLUMN publisher_id int;

UPDATE books_simple
SET publisher_id = (
    SELECT publishers.id
    FROM publishers
    WHERE publishers.publisher = books_simple.publisher);

ALTER TABLE books_simple DROP COLUMN publisher;
```

Note: you *may* look up the book ID (8909) here and use that instead of the title in the WHERE clause.

6.1
```
SELECT *
FROM books_simple, publishers
WHERE books_simple.title = "The War of the Worlds"
  AND publishers.id = books_simple.publisher_id;
```

6.2
```
SELECT *
FROM books_simple, publishers, languages
WHERE books_simple.title = "The War of the Worlds"
  AND publishers.id = books_simple.publisher_id
  AND languages.id = books_simple.language_id;
```

6.3
```
SELECT b.title,b.authors,l.language,p.publisher
FROM books_simple AS b,languages AS l, publishers AS p
WHERE b.Title = 'The War of the Worlds'
  AND b.language_id = l.id
  AND b.publisher_id = p.id;
```

Printed in Great Britain
by Amazon